P9-AQF-423

Modern Industrial World

South Africa

David Flint

RSVP
RAINTREE
STECK-VAUGHN
PUBLISHERS
The Steck-Vaughn Company

Austin, Texas

MODERN INDUSTRIAL WORLD

Australia	**Portugal**
Canada	**Russia**
France	**South Africa**
Germany	**Spain**
Japan	**Sweden**

Cover: The city of Cape Town, with Table Mountain in the background
Title page: A towering modern office skyscraper alongside traditional architecture in Johannesburg's mix of new and old
Contents page: The steep, arid slopes of the Drakensburg Mountains are a formidable challenge to walkers.

© **Copyright 1997, text, Steck-Vaughn Company**

All rights reserved. No part of this book may be reproduced or utilized in any form or by any means, electronic or mechanical, including photocopying, recording, or by any information storage and retrieval system, without permission in writing from the Publisher. Inquiries should be addressed to: Copyright Permissions, Steck-Vaughn Company, P.O. Box 26015, Austin, TX 78755.

Published by Raintree Steck-Vaughn Publishers,
an imprint of Steck-Vaughn Company

Library of Congress Cataloging-in-Publication Data
Flint, David.
South Africa / David Flint.
    p.   cm.—(Modern industrial world)
    Includes bibliographical references and index.
    Summary: While surveying many aspects of this country which has undergone major changes since 1993, this work emphasizes its natural resources, industry, and economy.
    ISBN 0-8172-4554-5
    1. South Africa—Juvenile literature.
    2. South Africa—Economic conditions—Juvenile literature.
    [1. South Africa. 2. South Africa—Economic conditions.]
    I. Title. II. Series.
    DT1787.F59 1996
    968—dc20   95-43250

Printed in Italy
1 2 3 4 5 6 7 8 9 0 01 00 99 98 97

Contents

Introduction   4

The Physical Environment   6

The People of South Africa   10

Farming, Forestry, and Fishing   16

Mining, Minerals, and Energy   22

Industry   27

Daily Life   31

Transportation, Tourism, and Trade   38

The Future   44

Glossary   46

Further Information   47

Index   48

Introduction

Voting in the 1994 South African elections. The right to vote for everyone over 18, and of any race, only came to South Africa for the first time that year. Thousands of polling stations had to be set up, often in remote, rural areas.

South Africa lies at the southern tip of the African continent, with the Atlantic Ocean to the west and the Indian Ocean to the east. It has 1,836 miles of coastline and is divided into nine provinces. To the north the country has frontiers with Namibia, Botswana, Zimbabwe, and Mozambique. South Africa also shares borders with the countries of Lesotho and Swaziland.

Until recently South Africa was ruled by a minority of white people. Only in 1993 did the black population achieve equal political rights with the white population. Since then, there have been major changes in all aspects of South African life, from schools, hospitals, and farms to factories and housing.

South Africa was divided into nine provinces by its new government in 1994.

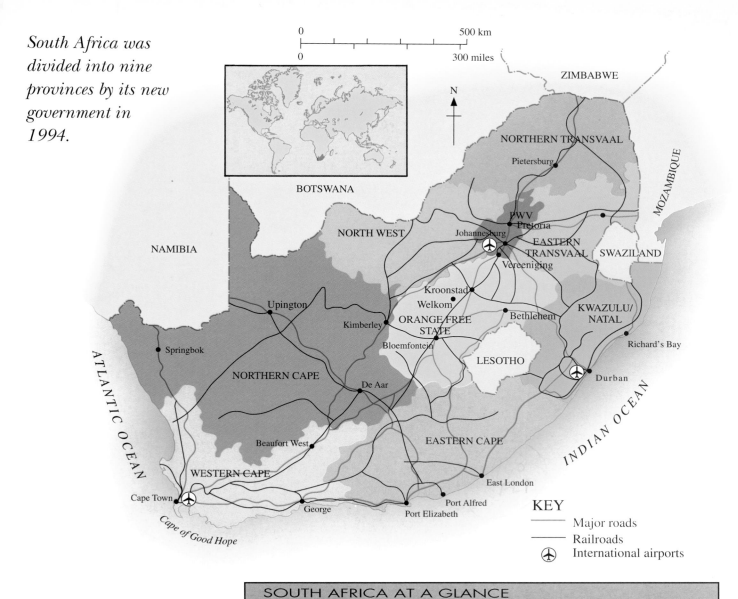

0   500 km
0   300 miles

N

ZIMBABWE

NORTHERN TRANSVAAL

Pietersburg

BOTSWANA

MOZAMBIQUE

NORTH WEST

PWV
Pretoria
Johannesburg
EASTERN
TRANSVAAL
Vereeniging
SWAZILAND

NAMIBIA

Kroonstad
Welkom
Bethlehem
KWAZULU/
NATAL

Upington
Kimberley
ORANGE FREE
STATE
Richard's Bay

Springbok
Bloemfontein
LESOTHO

NORTHERN CAPE
De Aar
Durban

ATLANTIC OCEAN

INDIAN OCEAN

Beaufort West

EASTERN CAPE

WESTERN CAPE
East London

Cape Town
Port Alfred
George
Port Elizabeth

Cape of Good Hope

KEY
—— Major roads
—— Railroads
✈ International airports

South Africa also includes the former homelands of Transkei, Bophuthatswana, Venda, and Ciskei. These were areas set up in the 1970s and 1980s as supposedly independent states by the former white government. In 1994, they became fully integrated into South Africa once again.

SOUTH AFRICA AT A GLANCE	
Area:	472,359 square miles
Population:	45 million
Population density:	95 people per square mile
Capital:	Pretoria
Infant mortality:	46 deaths per 1,000 births
Language:	11 official languages, of which Zulu, Xhosa, Afrikaans, Sepedi, English, and Setswana have the most speakers.
Currency:	The Rand (R)
Highest mountain:	Makheke (11,355 feet)
Longest river:	Orange (1,305 miles)

Source: *South African Yearbook*, 1994

The Physical Environment

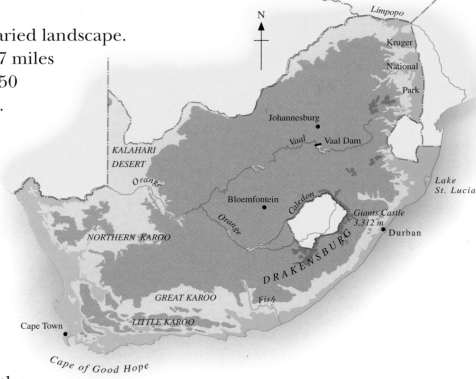

Land height scale bar: 0 to 500 km / 0 to 300 miles

Map labels: Limpopo, Kruger National Park, Johannesburg, Vaal, Vaal Dam, KALAHARI DESERT, Orange, Lake St. Lucia, Bloemfontein, Caledon, Giants Castle 3,312 m, Durban, Orange, NORTHERN KAROO, DRAKENSBURG, GREAT KAROO, Fish, Cape Town, LITTLE KAROO, Cape of Good Hope, N

South Africa has a rich and varied landscape. The flat coastal plain is only 37 miles wide in the west and between 50 and 150 miles wide in the east. Inland from this coastal plain the land rises steeply in the mountainous ranges of the Great Escarpment. The Drakensburg ("Dragon's Teeth") Mountains form one of the highest parts of this escarpment, rising to over 8,250 feet. Inland from the escarpment is the gently rolling interior plateau called the veld, given its name by Dutch settlers in the nineteenth century (*veld* is Dutch for *field*). The veld is a vast, grassy plain some 6,000 feet above sea level. It is dotted with farms, sheep stations, and national parks.

LAND HEIGHT

	Land under 165 ft
	165–3,300 ft
	3,300–6,600 ft
	Land over 6,600 ft

Cathedral Peak is on the wetter, eastern side of the Drakensburg Mountains. Here, winds sweeping in from the Indian Ocean bring rain clouds that pile up against the mountains, watering the whole landscape.

CLIMATE AND WEATHER HAZARDS

There is a big difference between the eastern and western parts of South Africa. The west is dryer, with parts of the northwest merging into the Kalahari Desert. The east gets more rain, carried in on winds from the Indian Ocean. However, because most of this rain falls in the summer, much of it evaporates so quickly that it never reaches the vegetation.

Over 65 percent of South Africa gets less than 20 inches of rain per year. This means that much of the country is dry. To make things worse, the rainfall is unreliable and unpredictable, so it varies a lot from year to year. Drought is quite common, rivers dry up, and the whole landscape turns brown.

Apart from drought, South Africa suffers other weather hazards. Tropical cyclones sweep in from the Indian Ocean and cause great damage, especially along the east coast. In contrast to the cyclones, tornadoes, which consist of funnels of air about four hundred feet wide, form over land, with winds in the funnel reaching speeds of over two hundred m.p.h. In 1993, a tornado killed seven people in the towns of Utrecht and Glencoe on the east coast. Because the interior plateau is six thousand feet above sea level, temperatures are cooler than in surrounding areas. This means that frosts can damage crops on clear, cold winter nights.

CLIMATE			
	Average daily temp.		Annual average rainfall
	January	July	
Johannesburg	65°F	60°F	30 inches
Durban	76°F	65°F	40 inches

"First the chickens die: there is no chaff from the grain. Then the dogs die: there are no scraps from the cooking pot. Then the goats die: there are no leaves they can reach…This is a hungry year."
—*from* **This Is a Hungry Year in South Africa by Gordon Ash, 1993**

Lake beds, like this one in Natal, crack and dry out in years of drought as the water disappears.

VEGETATION AND WILDLIFE

Because so much of South Africa is dry, the main vegetation is grassland. In the west, where desert and semidesert conditions prevail, even the grass cannot survive. Here there are a few cacti salt bushes and some coarse grasses. Animals such as the bat-eared fox, jackal, and ostrich are adapted to live in this hot, dry environment. Further east is the area of mixed grassland and trees called the Bushveld. Here trees like the baobab, candelabra, and monkey thorn thrive. Wild fruit trees in the Bushveld attract birds such as hornbills, shrikes, and flycatchers and animals such as lions, leopards, elephants, rhinoceroses, zebras, kudu, and giraffes.

Areas with heavier rainfall, such as the east coast, have forests of yellowwood and ironwood trees as well as pines, firs, and larches. Natural forests are home to colorful birds such as the Cape parrot and the rameron pigeon as well as the endangered samango monkey and the bushpig.

The Western Cape has a Mediterranean type of climate with warm, wet winters and hot, dry summers. Here there are drought-resistant shrubs such as rosemary, thyme, and heather as well as a few trees like the cork oak and the vine, which have long roots that reach water deep underground.

South Africa has been described as "the greatest wildlife show on earth" because of the number and variety of its wildlife. Of the world's land mammals, South Africa has the three biggest (the elephant, white rhino, and hippopotamus), the tallest (giraffe), the fastest (cheetah), and the smallest (pygmy shrew). There are also 160 species of snakes and 230 species of reptiles (including crocodiles).

There are now many more herds of giraffe than 15 or 20 years ago. Their numbers have increased thanks to South Africa's game parks, where the animals are protected. Unfortunately, as giraffe numbers grow, damage to trees becomes more widespread.

RIVERS

The Orange River is the major river in South Africa. With its
tributaries, the Vaal and the Caledon, it flows westward
across much of the country. Although impressive on a map,
the western part of the Orange River is almost dry for most
of the year since so much water evaporates in the desert.
However, farther east it provides vital water for irrigated
farming as well as for hydroelectric power.

*The Orange River
flows in this gorge for
250 miles of its course
as it nears the sea, in
the hot, desert region of
the northwest.*

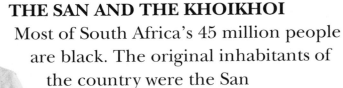

The People of South Africa

THE SAN AND THE KHOIKHOI

Most of South Africa's 45 million people are black. The original inhabitants of the country were the San (sometimes called Bushmen) and the Khoikhoi (or Hottentots). Today there are less than 40,000 of these people left in the country. However, before 1500 there were many more, and they were a nomadic people who roamed across the whole area south of the Zambezi River. Of the remaining San and Khoikhoi today, most live in the dry, western areas on the edge of the desert. They still live a nomadic life, moving from place to place gathering fruit and nuts for food and hunting animals such as the antelope using spears, bows, and arrows. Like their ancestors, the San and Khoikhoi are highly skilled at surviving in desert conditions. They can find water deep underground and use empty ostrich eggs to store water.

Xhosa men, wearing warm, woolen clothing. The Xhosa people mostly live in the Eastern Cape, where nighttime temperatures can fall below freezing. There are 18 different click sounds in the Xhosa language.

THE NGUNI

In the fourteenth and fifteenth centuries, Bantu-speaking groups of people moved into South Africa from the north and pushed the San and Koikhoi westward. The largest of these groups were the Nguni, who now make up two-thirds of the entire black population of South Africa. The Nguni speak a wide range of languages, such as Xhosa, Zulu, and Swazi. Despite their differences, people can still understand each other's language.

10

OTHER GROUPS

The Sotho-Tswana are a second group of people who live in the central region of South Africa. Their languages have a long cultural tradition but are very different from the Nguni languages. Two other main groups of people who also arrived in South Africa in the fourteenth and fifteenth centuries are the Tsonga, who live in the western parts of the country, and the Venda, who live near the Limpopo River.

LANGUAGE GROUPS
(millions)

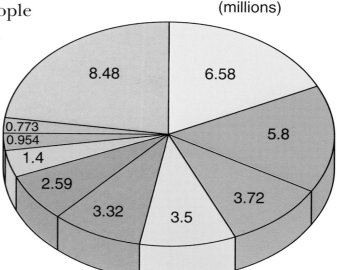

8.48
6.58
5.8
0.773
0.954
1.4
2.59
3.32
3.5
3.72

KEY

	Zulu
	Xhosa
	Afrikaans
	North Sotho
	English
	Tswana
	South Sotho
	Shangaan-Tsonga
	Swazi
	Ndebele & Venda

Source: Reuter

WHITE SETTLERS

In the seventeenth century, white people arrived by sea from Europe. In 1652, the Dutch East India Company set up a small settlement in the Cape area to act as a place to refuel on the sea route to India. By 1795, more than 15,000 Dutch people had settled in the area. The Dutch called themselves Boers, which means farmers.

During the Napoleonic Wars of 1795–1815, Great Britain occupied the Cape and established its rule. British explorers and settlers began to arrive in the 1800s. Since relations between the British and Dutch were never very good, in 1836, the Dutch moved inland and eastward in what is called the Great Trek, to escape British rule. As the white population grew they spread inland, taking land from the black African people.

When gold was discovered in South Africa's interior, the British and Dutch settlers both mined and fought over the riches. Most black people were controlled by the whites and worked on farms or in mines. In 1910, South Africa became part of the British Empire and remained a member of the Commonwealth until 1961, when it became a white-dominated republic.

An early photograph, taken in 1901, of Boer farmers outside a farmhouse. The Boers were Dutch settlers, whose dislike of British settlers flared in the Boer War of 1899–1902.

11

ASIAN IMMIGRANTS

South Africa's first Indian people were Hindus from Madras, who arrived in 1860. They came to work as laborers on the British sugar plantations along the east coast. Later in 1902, a shortage of miners led to the arrival of Chinese laborers in the country.

APARTHEID AND AFTER

From the 1820s until 1994, South Africa was ruled by white Dutch and British settlers and their descendants. They formed separate communities and married mostly among themselves. Black people were not allowed to vote and had to work in white-owned factories, farms, mines, shops, and offices. In the 1950s, the white South African Government introduced a policy called apartheid, which means "apartness" in Afrikaans, the language of Dutch settlers. Under this policy, black people had very few rights. They were forced to travel on different buses, go to different schools, even to sit on separate park benches from white people. They had to live either in separate townships near the cities or in homelands. The homelands were set up in the 1970s as parts of the country where black people of the same tribe were forced to live.

An African National Congress (ANC) rally in Soweto, in 1989. The ANC is a political organization that has campaigned for equal rights for black people since its foundation in 1912. For many years the ANC was banned by the government, but supporters still met and planned for the future.

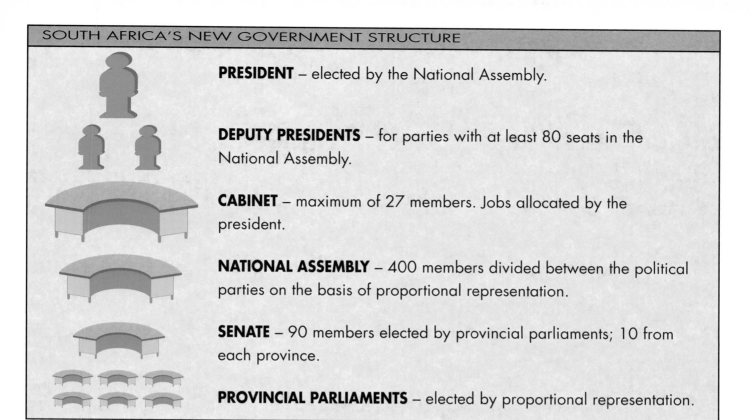

PRESIDENT – elected by the National Assembly.

DEPUTY PRESIDENTS – for parties with at least 80 seats in the National Assembly.

CABINET – maximum of 27 members. Jobs allocated by the president.

NATIONAL ASSEMBLY – 400 members divided between the political parties on the basis of proportional representation.

SENATE – 90 members elected by provincial parliaments; 10 from each province.

PROVINCIAL PARLIAMENTS – elected by proportional representation.

Nelson Mandela, soon after his release from prison in 1990, making the victory salute.

Blacks could only live near towns if they worked there. The homelands were supposed to be self-governing countries. However, they were controlled by the white South African Government, who saw them as places that confined black people to stop them from taking over the country.

Throughout the 1970s and 1980s, black people rebelled against the white government many times. Nelson Mandela became a symbol of the fight for black civil rights and majority rule. Trained as a lawyer, Mandela was an organizer of the African National Congress (ANC), one of the early black political organizations. He was imprisoned in 1964 for his political activities but was finally released in 1990. By this time the white government had started to negotiate with black leaders to end apartheid. The process took four years, but eventually, in April 1994, all South Africans were able to vote in free elections for the first time. Nelson Mandela was elected as the new president, and the ANC became the largest political party.

13

Mandela takes the oath of office as he is sworn in as President of South Africa, after winning the 1994 elections.

1994 Elected President of South Africa.

1993 Mandela and President Frederik W. de Klerk win the Nobel Peace Prize.

1956 Mandela is one of 156 people who are sent to prison for plotting to overthrow the government.

1964 Sentenced to life imprisonment for plotting to overthrow the government.

1951 Elected President of the ANC in the Transvaal region.

1990 February 11: Mandela is released after 28 years in prison.

1948 The all-white national party comes to power and begins apartheid.

1930 Goes to school, where books told of white heroes and Africans who were "savages."

1960 Mandela is released. Forms a wing of the ANC to bomb buildings that symbolize white South African rule.

1952 Imprisoned for not having a late-night pass.

1949 Mandela is put in charge of the Youth League of the ANC.

The last photograph of Mandela taken before he went to prison in 1964

1918 July 8: Nelson Mandela is born. Nelson is his European name. Rolihahla is his Xhosa name.

POPULATION DENSITY

Most people in South Africa live in one of the four main industrial areas around the cities of Johannesburg, Durban, Port Elizabeth, and Cape Town shown on the map. These areas in total make up only four percent of South Africa's land area, but they are home to over one-third of its people. In the past, most South Africans lived in the countryside, but in the last few years more and more people have been moving into large towns and cities. By 1995, nearly 55 percent of all South Africans lived in cities. By the year 2000, out of a total population of 45 million, at least 65 percent are predicted to live in towns.

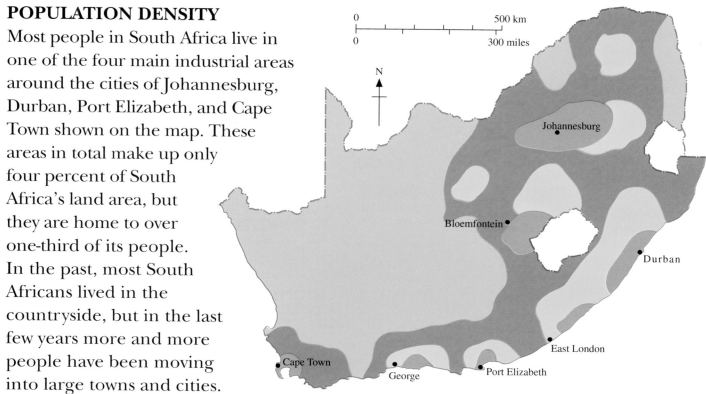

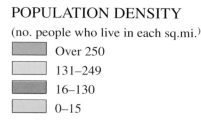

POPULATION DENSITY
(no. people who live in each sq.mi.)

- Over 250
- 131–249
- 16–130
- 0–15

South Africa's population is also very young—almost 37 percent are under 15 years of age. A further 59 percent are aged between 15 and 64 years old, and only 4 percent are over 65. However, there are big differences in how long South Africans can expect to live. On average, white women can expect to live 77 years and white men 70 years, but black South African men can only expect to live 64 years and black women 67 years. These differences are the result of the poorer health services, housing, and other services available to black South Africans. The former apartheid system had channeled government money to whites in preference to other population groups, and this led to inequalities in access to public services like clean water and sanitation. However, since 1994, the government has made great efforts to reduce some of these inequalities (see pages 31–35).

*"So far we have not solved the problem of how to keep people down on the farm after they've seen Johannesburg. So there's a huge wave of mostly young people quitting the countryside in the hope of better things in the cities. But who is going to grow the food?"—**Winky Timiya, South African businessman***

15

Farming, Forestry, and Fishing

There are two main types of farming in South Africa: commercial farming, which sells produce (often abroad) to make money; and subsistence farming, which only grows enough food to feed the people who farm the land. Commercial farming is very important in South Africa, providing nearly 7 percent of all the country's exports. It also employs over one million people. However, subsistence farms cover large parts of the countryside and employ between two and three million people. They grow corn and vegetables and usually keep a few animals such as cows, chickens, or pigs. These small farms and the villages they support in the countryside are a vital part of South Africa's agriculture. Since 1994, the government has been trying to help these farmers by organizing them into cooperatives and by increasing their credit to buy better seed and higher quality animals.

"At the moment we grow enough food both to feed most of our people and to sell some abroad. But I worry about the future. We need all the land we've got to grow more food for more South Africans. So I think we might have to stop growing export crops and concentrate on food."
—Jay Naidos, senior minister in the South African Government

Women working on their vegetable gardens in the Northern Transvaal. Here, water is the vital ingredient for successful farming, and the women have to carry it in buckets and drums from the river.

SOUTH AFRICA'S AGRICULTURAL REGIONS

Only 13 percent of South Africa is suitable for farming. The rest is too high, too steep, and too dry. However, research and better farm management have doubled the production of agriculture (mainly commercial farming) in the last 20 years. Because so much of the country is dry, irrigated farming along the Orange River is extremely important. Here, large dams store water that irrigates 2.5 million acres of land. Irrigated land is expensive, so only valuable crops such as sugar, citrus fruits, tropical fruits, and grain are grown on it.

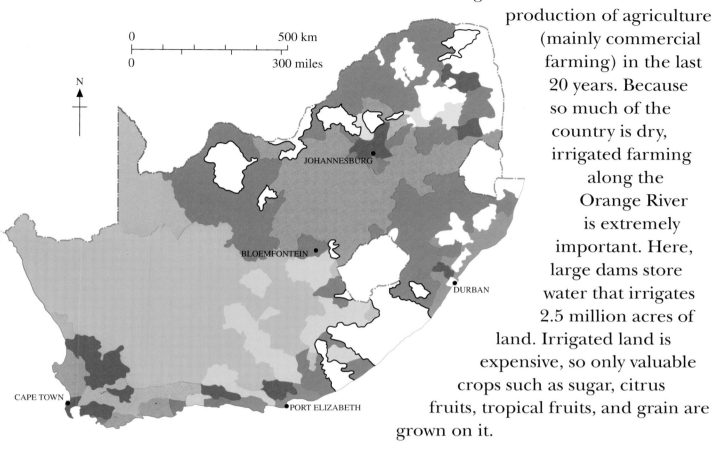

AGRICULTURAL REGIONS
(main agricultural produce sold per district)

- Cereal
- Sugarcane
- Other mixed crops
- Vegetables
- Forestry
- Fruit
- Grapes
- Beef cattle
- Dairy
- Mutton/lamb
- Wool
- Karakul sheep
- Poultry/eggs
- Other livestock
- No data

CEREAL CROPS

Corn is one of South Africa's main cereal crops, although large-scale production did not begin until the nineteenth century. Since corn cannot tolerate drought, it is grown in the eastern parts of the country and on irrigated land. It is used to feed both humans and animals, and a surplus is exported.

Wheat and barley are mostly grown in the Western Cape area. They are used to produce flour for bread, but a little is turned into cattle food. Wheat tends to be grown on larger farms that have big machines such as combine harvesters. These farms also spread lots of artificial fertilizer on the soil to get a good yield of the crop. Barley is used in the brewing industry as well as to produce food for pigs, sheep, and cattle.

17

SUGARCANE

South Africa is the world's tenth-largest sugar producer. Sugarcane looks like a very tall grass (up to ten feet high) and originally came from southern Asia. Sugarcane is mostly grown in the southeast, but a new area has also developed on the irrigated land along the Orange River.

TOBACCO AND COTTON

There are more than one thousand tobacco growers in South Africa, producing about 36,300 tons of tobacco a year. In total, South Africa is able to produce 173 different grades of Virginia tobacco and five grades of Oriental tobacco.

Cotton is another important crop because it supplies the raw material for the cotton mills. Production has increased in recent years since more artificial fertilizer has been used to give higher yields.

Sugarcane is harvested by hand.

FRUIT

Much of South Africa's fruit, especially apples, pears, and grapes, is exported to markets in Europe, and Cape fruit is famous worldwide. The big expansion of fruit-growing came during the twentieth century with the development of cold storage and refrigerated trucks and ships. These changes made export possible. Tropical fruits such as mangoes, bananas, guanas, macadamia nuts, and pecans have recently dominated fruit farming in the subtropical coasts of the Eastern Cape and Natal.

CROP PRODUCTION, 1993	
	(million tons)
Sugarcane	14.2
Corn	9.7
Wheat	1.4
Deciduous fruits (apples, pears, plums)	1.1
Citrus fruits	1.0
Sunflower seeds	0.41
Subtropical fruits	0.42
Sorghum	0.04

ORNAMENTAL PLANTS

South Africa is a major producer of ornamental plants, including cut flowers and potted plants. Most are sent to Europe, including roses, gladiolas, chrysanthemums, and the protea, a special South African native flower that has become very popular. This relatively new industry employs 15,000 people, and as overseas markets expand, this figure will grow.

WINE

Over 250,000 acres of land are covered by wine grapes, and South Africa has become a major exporter of wine and brandy. In 1992, South Africa produced four percent of the world's wine, but this figure is growing fast. Some grapes are dried and exported as raisins, sultanas, and currants.

The grape harvest is vital to the prosperity of South Africa. Vineyards like these need many people to care for them, especially at pruning, planting, weeding, and harvest times.

GOATS AND MOHAIR

South Africa produces nearly half of the total world production of mohair from its Angora goats. This fine, high-quality wool is exported for use in sweaters and high fashion clothes all over the world. Over four thousand Angora farmers keep 2.5 million goats, mostly in the Cape area.

SHEEP AND WOOL

South Africa has over 26 million sheep that are reared for their wool and their meat. Sheep were first introduced into South Africa from Europe in 1654 by the Dutch East India Company. Now South Africa is a major exporter of high-quality sheep's wool.

CATTLE

There are over eight million cattle in South Africa, some on large commercial farms, others on much smaller subsistence farms. Cattle are reared for milk near the main industrial centers such as Pretoria/Witwatersrand/Vereeniging (PWV), and the Cape area. However, there are large cattle ranches in the western parts of the country, where the heavier rain helps to grow better grass and allows fodder crops such as corn, beans, and peanuts to be grown.

Cattle are rounded up for branding in Natal. Most cattle ranches are large, covering hundreds or even thousands of acres.

SOUTH AFRICA'S ANIMALS, 1993	
	(millions)
Sheep	25.6
Hens	10.7
Cattle	8.1
Goats	2.5
Pigs	1.2

FORESTRY

Only 2.3 percent of South Africa is covered by forest, but over 1,100 species of trees grow along the south and east coasts and in parts of the interior. The yellow-wood tree is the country's national tree and often grows to over 130 feet tall. Many of South Africa's forests were cut down in the nineteenth century, but the government has recently started plantations to reforest large areas. By 1994, four million acres of land were covered by forests planted by the government. As a result of these plantations, South Africa can produce most of the timber it needs, as well as export some newsprint, lumber, and wood pulp.

The government is still eager to expand the area planted with trees, especially in remote regions, so that local people will be able to use the lumber for firewood and for building.

The Fishing Industry

From its 1,836 miles of coastline, in 1993 South Africa harvested 692,000 tons of fish and shellfish. About 27,000 people work in the fishing industry, either on boats out at sea or onshore processing the fish. Over 90 percent of the catch comes from the cold waters off the western coast. The government has a strict conservation policy in a fishing zone of two hundred nautical miles from the shore. This sets quotas, or limits, to the number of fish that are allowed to be caught. The quotas were reduced in the early 1990s because fish numbers were declining.

"To most people South Africa means gold, diamonds, or grapes. But we have a proud history of fishing."
—Ngoaka Sexwale, Director of the Sea Fisheries Research Institute, Department of Environment Affairs

However, by 1993 there was some recovery. Anchovies, pilchards, and herring are processed into fish meal, fish oil, and canned fish. Hake and sole are the main fish caught by trawling. Lobsters are also important, as 75 percent are exported.

A Japanese trawler's catch is unloaded in Cape Town. The amount of fish such boats can catch in South African waters is limited by the government.

Mining, Minerals, and Energy

South Africa's valuable mineral wealth has sped up its economic development. The main minerals are gold, diamonds, uranium, coal, copper, and tin. According to a recent survey, South Africa is the world's largest producer of gold, platinum, chrome ore, manganese, vanadium, and vermiculite and the world's second largest producer of titanium and zircon. It is also the world's fifth largest producer of diamonds. In 1993, mineral exports made up 48 percent of all South Africa's exports, so they are vital to its development. Most of South Africa's minerals are mined by large private companies, such as the Anglo-American Corporation or Anglovaal. About half a million workers are employed in the mines.

Miners drill long holes into the Gold Reef, seven thousand feet below the surface in the Transvaal. At such depths the temperature is over 80°F and working conditions are cramped and dangerous.

GOLD MINING

South Africa, mines more than six hundred tons of gold each year, which is 28 percent of the total world production. Gold is the country's main earner of foreign currency, and in 1993 gold made up 61 percent of all South Africa's exports.

Today the goldfields form an arc about 260 miles long stretching across the Transvaal and the Orange Free State. The first goldfield was discovered in 1886. The new village of Johannesburg had grown up, and land was being offered for sale. Since then, Johannesburg has grown to a giant city of 1.9 million people.

SOUTH AFRICA'S PRECIOUS MINERALS			
	1988	1990	1993
Gold production	682 tons	665 tons	680 tons
Diamonds (in carats)	9,115,880	8,713,527	10,622,403

South Africa's gold is mined by sinking deep shafts to reach gold-bearing rocks called reefs. The reefs are narrow and cannot support large machines, so gold mining requires many workers. Pneumatic drills drill out the rock and crush it to chips. The chips are ground to a pulp and the gold is extracted from the pulp using cyanide. For every ounce of gold, three or four tons of rock have to be dug out of the ground.

ENERGY IN SOUTH AFRICA

South Africa mines coal to burn in power stations to generate electricity. In 1993, 145 million tons of coal were used within South Africa, and 57 million tons were exported. This makes coal the second most valuable export after gold. Some coal is used to make synthetic oil.

Although South Africa covers only four percent of the continent of Africa and has just six percent of its people, the country generates over half of all electricity in Africa. Only about 12 million South Africans have electricity in their homes, but the government aims to make this 30 million people by the year 2000. South Africa has one nuclear power station (see pages 44–45) that uses uranium to generate electricity.

Liquid gold is poured into ingots after being heated with cyanide. The cyanide separates the gold from the impurities in the pulp.

DIAMONDS

In 1867, a pebble on the banks of the Orange River was identified as a diamond, and in 1871, the diamond field of Kimberley was discovered. Diamonds are found in rocks called pipes, which are the remains of old volcanoes. At first, diamonds were mined close to the surface in huge pits. But now miners have to go deep underground to reach the diamonds. Some diamonds are washed out of the rock by rivers and transported to the sea. These can be found along riverbeds or along the coast near the mouth of the Orange River. South Africa is now the world's fifth-largest producer of diamonds.

When they are first mined, the diamonds look like pebbles. It is only when they are cut that they sparkle. Diamond cutting is a highly skilled job. The cutters try to create lots of different angles that reflect light back through the diamond.

Diamonds are weighed in carats. One carat is equal to 200 milligrams. The largest diamond ever found was the Cullinan diamond, which weighed three thousand carats before it was cut up. The Star of Africa, a diamond as big as a golf ball, was the largest gem cut from the Cullinan diamond. The Star of Africa is now in the Royal Sceptre of the British Crown Jewels.

The former Kimberley mine, called The Big Hole, is now a national monument. It is the largest artificial hole in the world. In 1869 it was just a hill, but diamond hunters dug out the ground to create a hole 2,500 feet deep, which is now flooded. A museum of the history of diamond mining has been built on the site.

Opposite The Big Hole, a former diamond mine at Kimberley. The immensity of the hole can be seen by comparing it to the height of the buildings in the background.

Below These uncut diamonds were dredged from the seabed on South Africa's west coast. Huge dredgers vacuum sediment from the seabed, which is then filtered and washed to separate the diamonds.

Miners and Their Families

In 1993 there were 950 mines in South Africa, with 17 training centers at gold, coal, and other mines. Many of the miners are men who have left their homes in other parts of South Africa or who have come from other countries. They are attracted by the chance of a permanent job with high wages. Many come to work in the mines for six months or a year before returning to their families for two to three months. Others move to the mines with their whole families. So mining companies provide houses in camps for about one million people. Miners and their families are also eligible for hospital care, clinics, and sporting facilities provided by the companies.

However, mining is a difficult and dangerous job. Conditions in a mine are often cramped, hot, and dangerous, and every year, 30 to 40 miners or more are killed. White workers still have higher pay and better jobs than black workers, but the new government is slowly trying to improve conditions for black workers.

A mining camp at an asbestos mine. These huts are lived in for six to nine months at a time while the asbestos is mined.

"Conditions in the mines are hot, dirty, dusty, and dangerous. There are few real safety precautions and everyone knows it might be his last look at the sunshine when that cage door closes. But we need the money and there is no work. So what else can we do?"
—*Josef Molefe, retired South African miner, 1994*

Industry

South Africa has become a major industrial world power. It is the most industrialized country within Africa and is expected to become wealthier from its industry. Industry generates more wealth for the country than agriculture, forestry, fishing, or even mining. The wide range of industries includes iron, steel, and car production and the manufacture of jewelry, carpets, and clothes.

IRON AND STEEL

South Africa is now the largest producer of iron and steel in Africa. Some of the steel is exported to more than 80 countries from ports such as Durban.

ISCOR is the Iron and Steel Company of South Africa. The iron and steel industry grew up in order to make equipment for the gold mines around Johannesburg. Since then, iron- and steelmaking have spread to Pretoria, Vereeniging, and Newcastle.

A worker tends to the blast furnace inside an ISCOR steel factory. The furnaces produce great heat, dust, and noise as they convert iron ore, coke, and limestone into steel. The workers need protective clothing when dealing with red-hot, molten steel.

ENGINEERING INDUSTRIES

South Africa has gained a reputation as a manufacturer of ships, railroad locomotives, cars, and aircraft. Steel produced by ISCOR was used to build machines for the country's gold and diamond mines. Later, railroad locomotives, wagons, and ships were built to carry exports of coal and minerals. Most recently, the South African Motor Corporation (SAMCAR) opened the country's most modern vehicle plant in Pretoria. Here, 23 robots assemble Ford, Mazda, and Mitsubishi cars with very little human help. South Africa also makes tractors and combine harvesters, as well as radios and television sets.

The country's electronics industry is one of the world's fastest growing industries. It specializes in telecommunication systems and computers and is based in Pretoria.

CONSUMER GOODS

South Africa has always had a wide range of industries making products for local people. Food processing, such as flour milling and sugar refining, is one of the most important of these consumer goods industries. Pasta, rice, oats, and wheat are all produced from local crops for sale in local stores and supermarkets.

A clothing factory in Cape Town. South Africa now produces more than 70 percent of its own clothing.

The Lesotho Highlands Water Project

This project is the largest water-supply plan ever undertaken in Africa. It was started in 1993 as a joint venture between South Africa and Lesotho to use the heavy rain that falls on the hills of Lesotho. The water will be collected in dams in the mountains of Lesotho and piped into South Africa, mainly into the PWV industrial area. Here the growth of industry over the last 20 years, together with the expansion of cities such as Johannesburg, has created a huge demand for water. More than nine million people live in the area. Some of the water will also be used to irrigate crops like corn, cotton, tobacco, and fruit grown in the same area. As the water flows from Lesotho, it will be used to generate hydroelectricity, which will help the growth of industry in Lesotho. The first water from the project will reach South Africa in 1997.

The clothing industry is also important, employing over 125,000 people in 1,230 factories. With South Africa's rapidly growing population there is a ready market for inexpensive shirts, dresses, blouses, trousers, and jackets.

Other factories make household goods such as stoves, washers, refrigerators, and vacuum cleaners, as well as carpets, glass, and furniture. The plastics industry employs 20,000 people in seven hundred factories. It uses local coal and synthetic oil to make plastic that is used in everything from car bumpers to bottles.

This successful brewery produces beer from sorghum (a type of corn), to be sold all over the country.

COLA WARS

In 1994, the Pepsi Cola company announced it was returning to South Africa in a joint venture with local businesspeople. Pepsi had opened its first such African factory in 1948 but had withdrawn from the country in 1985 in protest against the apartheid policy. Since returning, Pepsi has opened a new factory to make half of the 275 million cases of soft drinks sold each year in South Africa. Now Pepsi and Coca-Cola are fighting for control of the growing South African market.

Richard Maponya

Sixty-four-year-old Richard Maponya is a legend in the township of Soweto, on the outskirts of Johannesburg. Maponya has become a millionaire over the past 40 years, and his business interests now include the BMW franchise, gas stations, stores, and property development. Born the son of a farmer, Maponya trained as a teacher before moving to Johannesburg, where he got a job as a clerk. Later he was promoted to become a buyer, but he could go no higher in the company because black people at that time were not allowed to be in higher positions than white people in business. Maponya started a dairy in 1952 and then a supermarket in Soweto. These were the beginning of his success.

"I am an ambitious man. I want to achieve. As a black man I was denied many things, but I set my goals, I kept going, and I never took no for an answer."
—*Richard Maponya, 1994*

30

Daily Life

EDUCATION

Until 1993, not all South African parents could send their children to school. Under the old apartheid system, all white children had to go to school, but nonwhite children did not. Public schools for nonwhite children were not as well equipped as those for whites, and many black children did not complete their secondary schooling. Even in 1992 the number of pupils per teacher was much higher in schools for nonwhite children. This meant that in some schools, classes of more than 50 children were common.

Since 1993, South Africa has been moving toward a single education system for all children where school attendance has been compulsory for all children from seven to sixteen years of age. Children are taught in their mother tongue, but they also study English or Afrikaans so that after their fifth year in school they can continue their studies at a higher level. In 1993, education was provided for 12 million students in 27,500 institutions.

This class, in a Cape Town township, has more than 50 children. Many teachers are now being trained to cut class sizes.

"There is a whole generation of black children who grew up with little or no schooling thanks to the apartheid system. I have friends of 25 who still cannot read or write. I want to know what the new government is doing for them."
—**Allan Mhlaba, resident of Crossroads Camp**

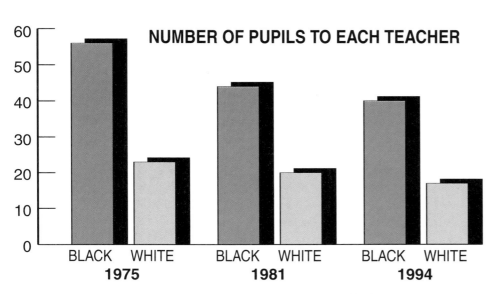

NUMBER OF PUPILS TO EACH TEACHER

BLACK WHITE
1975

BLACK WHITE
1981

BLACK WHITE
1994

The new government regards the improvement of education for its nonwhite children as one of its most important tasks. However, building new schools and training new teachers is an expensive process in a country where many people are still very poor. It is also estimated that up to 50 percent of the total population may be unable to read and write. Programs such as Operation Upgrade and Read are being started by the government to tackle this problem by helping adults learn how to read and write.

"The outside world can see that we are feeding no fewer than five million needy children free of charge, and we have introduced clean water and proper sewage disposal all over the country."
—**Nelson Mandela, May 23, 1995**

POPULATION GROWTH

South Africa has over 26,000 doctors, 4,000 dentists, 9,400 pharmacists, and 158,000 nurses. However, these will not be enough to cope with the rapidly growing population. In fact, over one million people are added to the total every year. The present population of 45 million will double in just 30 years' time. In order to slow down this population growth, the government has set up primary health care programs that include advice on family planning together with education and training programs.

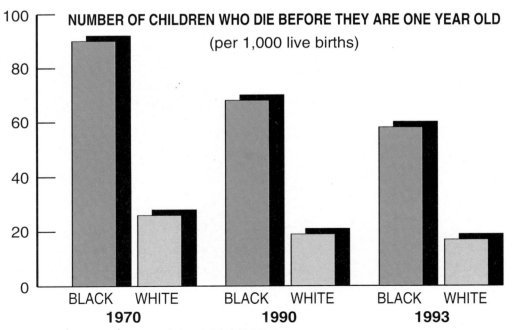

NUMBER OF CHILDREN WHO DIE BEFORE THEY ARE ONE YEAR OLD
(per 1,000 live births)

BLACK   WHITE
1970

BLACK   WHITE
1990

BLACK   WHITE
1993

Source: *The Guardian*, April 26, 1994 (SAIRR)

Left The falling infant mortality figures in South Africa have added to the country's population growth.

32

HEALTH

Until 1993, health standards were much higher among the white population than among the rest of the country's people. More money had been spent on hospitals, clinics, and doctors for white people than for everyone else. As a result, white people on average lived to 73 years of age, but everyone else lived to an average of 63 years. The government has been taking steps to improve the health care available to black South Africans by building new hospitals and training more doctors and nurses. However, the real problem is poverty. Black South Africans still tend to be poor and consequently have diets that leave them exposed to diseases such as tuberculosis, which kills 35 people every day. Damp, cold, and drafty housing is another condition that makes black South Africans more prone to illness.

At clinics like this one, mothers with young children get food and hygiene advice as well as health care.

HOUSING

Plans to improve the quality of housing for black South Africans have been a high priority since 1994. However, improving housing is a huge problem for the new South African Government for the following reasons:

- there is a backlog of at least 1.5 million houses needing improvement dating from the apartheid years;

- most people needing houses are poor and cannot afford to buy them;

- many people moved from the countryside into towns between 1990 and 1994 in search of better jobs. By 2010 it is estimated that 70 percent of South Africans will live in towns rather than the present 50 percent, so it appears that the problem will get worse;

- the government does not have much money to spend on housing because it is also trying to improve other areas of life such as schools, hospitals, and farms; and

- more than seven million South Africans live in squatter-type settlements, which often have no clean water, electricity, or sewage disposal. People build their own homes here out of any scrap materials they can find such as corrugated iron, plastic, and even cardboard.

New township houses being built as part of the government's massive house building program. Where possible, locally produced bricks and lumber are used to keep costs down and provide jobs for local people.

In order to overcome these problems, the South African government has set out to build 300,000 homes a year for the next ten years. This is not only expensive but is taking up large areas of land, often on the edge of major cities, such as Cape Town, Durban, and Johannesburg.

34

However, the building has created jobs for carpenters, electricians, laborers, and bricklayers. At the same time the government is improving the two hundred hostels where 400,000 migrant workers live.

"South Africa is a mixture of First and Third Worlds. The differences are based on race. Most white people live in the rich First World in South Africa. Most black people live in the poor Third World of the country."—**John Dixon, in Trade and Travel Magazine, 1995**

CONDITIONS IN THE COUNTRYSIDE

Many South Africans who live in the countryside live in villages consisting of traditional huts built around a central cattle kraal (pen) or meeting place. The huts are circular and built from local materials, such as mud and sticks. Roofs are thatched with local grass. Again, poverty is the main problem in trying to improve housing in the countryside. The government is trying to bring electricity to as many villages as possible and to help villagers sink new wells to get safe drinking water.

A Zulu house in the Natal countryside. Rural houses are built of local clays and muds that when mixed with straw can be baked in the sun to produce bricks. Small windows and thick walls help keep homes cool.

STORES AND MARKETS

Large towns and cities have stores and supermarkets where people buy food, clothing, and other household goods. However, the people who live in small towns and villages often shop in markets. These markets are very busy places packed with people buying, selling, and catching up on news with friends.

Most markets sell a wide range of goods, from vegetables and fruit to cloth and household goods such as pots and pans. Most of the fruits, such as oranges, grapes, and lemons, have been grown on small farms and are sold to boost the family income. Farmers also sell chickens, goats, sheep, and cattle that they have reared. Those markets near the coast also have stalls selling fresh fish and shellfish.

Markets sell a wide range of goods, from fruit and vegetables, such as the green mangoes and gourds above, to handmade baskets and bags.

FOOD

Corn is an important part of most people's diet. It is ground up and cooked as porridge, often with a beef stew. Meat does not stay fresh for very long in hot climates, so some is cured and dried. The meat is dried in the sun and cut into strips, called biltong. It will last a very long time, and though it is very chewy, it is nourishing.

Food from India is also found in many South African markets. One meal is called bunny chow. This is half a loaf of bread with its middle torn out and filled with curried meat.

36

MASS MEDIA

Most radio and television in South Africa today is controlled by the South African Broadcasting Corporation (SABC), although new independent commercial radio stations and a cable television service (M-Net) are growing fast.

South Africa has six national radio stations and six regional stations, together with eight stations for language groups, such as Radio Zulu. Every day, 14 million listeners tune in to SABC's stations.

There are three television stations offering services in nine languages. Channel TV1 transmits in English and Afrikaans, CCV transmits in Zulu, Xhosa, Hindi, Tamil, English, and Afrikaans, and TSS-TV focuses on sports and education. About 11 million adults watch television each day in South Africa, which gives it the largest audience in the continent of Africa. About half of all programs on South African television are made in South Africa itself, the rest being programs bought from the United States, Great Britain, and other countries.

South Africa's television and radio stations are vital to community life. Many homes now have radios, and there are 2.5 million homes with television sets. In country areas, people gather together around the television set at shops to watch their favorite soap operas and other programs.

SPORTS

Sports are very popular in South Africa, and more and more people are playing and going to see sports. The most popularly played sport is soccer, followed by netball, cricket, rugby, and golf. Soccer is also the sport that attracts the most spectators, followed by boxing, tennis, gymnastics, rugby, and cricket. Until 1991, South Africa was unable to take part in international sporting events because of the world's protest of its apartheid policy, which gave white people much better sports facilities than it gave to black people. Since then, the government has been spending more money on sports facilities for black people to encourage more to play national sports such as cricket, rugby, and soccer.

Transportation, Tourism, and Trade

TOURISM

South Africa has lots of attractions for tourists. The main attractions are:

- beautiful scenery, from Table Mountain in Cape Town to the broad, sandy Durban beaches and the craggy Drakensburg Mountains;
- a vast collection of some of the world's rarest and most stunning wildlife;
- some of the most interesting and spectacular cultures, customs, dance, and dress, such as the Zulu spears, shields, and dances or the basketware, clay pots, and wood carving of the Venda people;
- the opportunity to visit and take part in a wide range of activities such as rafting, boat trips, scuba diving, golf, balloon trips, and camel, elephant, and pony rides; and
- many hotels, game lodges, and bed and breakfast inns in which to stay.

The dramatic background of the Twelve Apostles in Cape Province. Areas of stunning natural beauty are just some of the attractions South Africa offers tourists.

Since 1986, the number of foreign tourists has grown from 300,000 a year to 650,000 in 1993. Tourism is already a major industry in South Africa, but it will become even bigger. Experts predict that by the year 2000, tourism in South Africa will replace gold as the country's major source of foreign currency.

Right Hikers in the Maluti Mountains, Rustlers Valley, enjoy the view.

Below Hotels in South Africa are given a number of stars by the South African Tourist Authority. Five-star hotels have every convenience; one-star hotels usually only offer shared bathrooms.

THE VALUE OF TOURISM

Tourism has created thousands of jobs, from taxi drivers to game wardens, chefs, waiters, and tour guides. Other jobs have been created in craft industries that make goods for the tourists, such as jewelry, glass, leather goods, and wood carvings.

Many foreign tourists come to visit relatives in South Africa. Others come to see the wildlife and the scenery. The fastest growing type of tourism is called ecotourism. Ecotourists are people who come to use the natural resources of scenery and wildlife without spoiling them. Ecotourists enjoy unharmful activities such as bird watching, photography, painting, snorkeling, hiking, or climbing. They often stay in tents or game parks and are organized so that they do not damage the environment or the wildlife of the area. South Africa has set up a network of 16 national parks, designed to preserve and protect areas of particularly important scenery and wildlife.

HOTELS IN SOUTH AFRICA

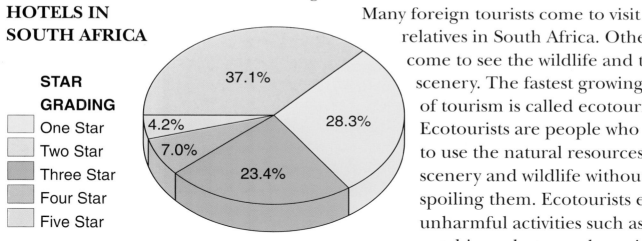

STAR GRADING
- One Star
- Two Star
- Three Star
- Four Star
- Five Star

37.1%
28.3%
4.2%
7.0%
23.4%

LOCATION
- Johannesburg
- Durban & Umhlanga
- Cape Peninsula
- Garden Route
- Witwatersrand & Vaal Triangle
- Other

50.1%
17.4%
13.3%
9.8%
4.7%
4.7%

Source: *Satour's Databank,* September, 1993

39

Kruger National Park

Kruger National Park, on the border with Mozambique, covers a huge area of eight thousand square miles. The park is home to a wide variety of different types of game. For example, there are 450 different types of birds in the park, 114 types of reptiles, and 40 different types of fish. However, the park's main attractions are its "Magnificent Seven"—namely rhinos, elephants, lions, leopards, buffalo, cheetahs, and wild dogs. The Park has 24 rest camps where up to six thousand people can stay in tents, trailers, or game lodges. Most people tour the park by car or safari bus to see and photograph the animals. There are also wilderness trails that people can visit on foot or on tours guided by rangers.

Above *Four-wheel drive vehicles allow tourists to get to remote parts of the national parks to photograph the wildlife. The park also provides jobs for local people as drivers and wardens.*

Left *The white rhinoceros, one of Kruger National Park's main attractions. Game wardens patrol the parks to protect the animals from poachers and to protect local crops and fields from the wildlife.*

41

TRANSPORTATION

South Africa has an extensive system of modern transportation run by Transnet Ltd., a large company employing 18,000 people and owned by the government. Transnet is made up of six main divisions:

- Spoornet, which covers the railroads;
- Autonet, which covers the roads;
- Portnet, which covers the ports;
- South African Airlines (SAA), which covers the airlines;
- Petronet, which covers the pipelines; and
- PX, which covers the parcel distribution.

There are over 36,000 miles of surfaced roads and 88,000 miles of unsurfaced roads in the country. The highway system links all the main cities to each other and to neighboring countries such as Zimbabwe and Mozambique.

RAILROADS

South Africa has 20,300 miles of railroad track, of which 11,000 miles is electrified. Railroads carry both freight and passengers. The majority of freight consists of heavy, bulky materials such as cement, coal, and iron ore. However, container traffic has grown recently, with over 370,000 containers being transported in 1993.

The Blue Train is a famous luxury passenger train that runs from Pretoria to Cape Town. There is also a network of commuter trains each day that carry 2.1 million people to and from work. This network is particularly important to the majority of South Africans, who do not own private cars. Commuting by rail is vital to the people who live in the townships on the edges of major cities.

South Africa has three international airports, at Johannesburg, Durban, and Cape Town. In addition, six regional airports make it possible to fly easily within the country.

Every working day, thousands of commuters use South Africa's trains to get to and from work. Railroads provide a relatively cheap, comfortable, and reliable way of traveling for most South Africans.

"The economy is in a bad state. It is very important that we rebuild our economy. We are looking to renew trade and to attract investment in South Africa."—Tom Manthata, a South African teacher, 1993

TRADE

South Africa's exports are dominated by gold, diamonds, and minerals. Other important exports include metals and fruit, flowers, and corn. The government is making a big effort to increase the export of manufactured goods. By 2010 it plans to export 10 percent of the total goods manufactured. South Africa imports mostly machinery, vehicles, chemicals, and other manufactured goods. Most of the country's imports come from Germany, the United States, Japan, and Great Britain. Switzerland is South Africa's biggest export market, followed by the U.S., Great

SOUTH AFRICA'S IMPORTS AND EXPORTS, 1993

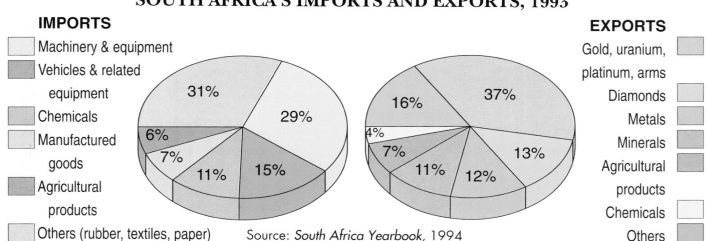

IMPORTS
- Machinery & equipment
- Vehicles & related equipment
- Chemicals
- Manufactured goods
- Agricultural products
- Others (rubber, textiles, paper)

31% 29% 6% 7% 11% 15%

EXPORTS
- Gold, uranium, platinum, arms
- Diamonds
- Metals
- Minerals
- Agricultural products
- Chemicals
- Others

16% 37% 4% 7% 13% 11% 12%

Source: *South Africa Yearbook,* 1994

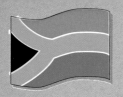

The Future

*"The rich countries like Japan, the United States, and Great Britain are lining up to buy our uranium, platinum, coal, and other minerals. In the past they got them cheaply but now they are going to have to pay a fair price for them."—**Mathew Phos, trade union official, 1994**

South Africa is already the most important industrial country within Africa. However, the country has huge potential for even further economic growth for four main reasons. First, South Africa still has enormous reserves of gold, diamonds, uranium, platinum, and other minerals. These will be valuable future exports, and new mineral deposits may be found. Second, South Africa's manufacturing industry already has a wide range, from textiles, food, and clothing to cars and chemicals. These industries are now set to expand while new industries, such as microcomputers, are gaining a foothold in the country. Third, good road, rail, and sea communications make it easy and cheap to move raw materials and finished goods around the country. Finally, South Africa has the ability to generate even more electricity as industry expands, from its coal and uranium and from its hydroelectric stations.

However, as part of this industrial growth it will be important for the government to raise living standards

South Africa is one of the world's nuclear powers with this plant at Pelindaba.

among the majority of its black population. In practice this means building better houses for people living in cramped townships. It also means providing electricity, clean water, and sewage disposal for people living in townships. One of the most important tasks facing the government is to create enough new jobs for the rapidly growing population. Jobs will also have to have reasonable rates of pay in order to provide people with the means to buy the things they need to live. Better schools, hospitals, and clinics are other important aims, together with increasing the number of adults who can read and write.

South Africa has enormous resources of people and raw materials to become a rich, successful nation. The challenge is to ensure that the wealth created by industrial growth benefits all South Africans, not just a minority.

Glossary

African National Congress (ANC) The main political party in South Africa, which was originally founded in 1912.

Afrikaans South African language based on Dutch. It is one of the country's official languages.

Apartheid A government policy of separate development for people of different races. White people got most of the country's wealth under apartheid, while nonwhite people suffered.

Artificial fertilizer Chemicals produced to speed up plant growth and used instead of natural manure.

Civil rights The freedoms, rights, and responsibilities that people should be able to enjoy in a democratic society.

Commonwealth The group of 51 countries that used to be British colonies and are now independent states. Commonwealth countries make up nearly a quarter of the world's population.

Consumer goods Things people buy as they become richer, such as television sets, stereos, washing machines, and automobiles.

Cyclones Circular tropical storms with very high winds and heavy rainfall. Cyclones can cause great destruction to homes, roads, factories, and farms.

Exports Goods produced by a country that are sold abroad. Exports may be goods like machinery, cars, clothes, fruits, and vegetables or services like banking and insurance.

Fodder crops Crops grown as food for animals. Barley and corn are two important fodder crops fed to cattle, sheep, and pigs.

Grain crops Crops that produce grains as seeds, such as wheat, barley, oats, and corn.

Hydroelectric power Electricity generated by the power of falling water.

Infrastructure The system of public works within a country, state, or city, such as bridges, water mains, etc.

Irrigation The controlled addition of water to soil in order to grow more crops.

Majority rule The election of a government by the majority of a country's people, not by a minority. Under majority rule, all adults are entitled to vote, irrespective of race, color, or religion.

Plankton Tiny organisms that live in the sea and that provide food for other sea creatures such as fish and squid.

Republic A form of government in which people are represented by elected officials.

Townships Poor areas on the edges of major cities. Many townships in South Africa do not have electricity or running water in homes.

Yield The amount of a particular crop or product produced at harvest. Fertilizers help to increase the yield of crops.

Further Information

Addresses

South African Embassy, 3051 Massachusetts Avenue NW, Washington, DC 20008

The South African Tourism Board, 500 Fifth Avenue, New York, NY 10110 can provide background information on South Africa. You can write to the board or call at (212) 730-2929.

State of the World's Children is an annual report with information on developing countries. Available from UNICEF, 1 UN Plaza, New York, NY 10017.

Further Reading

Halliburton, Warren J. *African Industries*. Africa Today. New York: Crestwood House, 1993.

Halliburton, Warren J. *African Landscapes*. Africa Today. New York: Crestwood House, 1993.

Hoobler, Dorothy and Hoobler, Thomas. *Mandela: The Man, the Struggle, the Triumph*. New York: Franklin Watts, 1992.

Hughes, Libby. *Nelson Mandela: Voice of Freedom*. People in Focus. New York: Dillon Press, 1992.

Meisel, Jacqueline Drobis. *South Africa at the Crossroads*. Headliners. Brookfield, CT: Millbrook Press, 1994.

Middleton, Nick. *Southern Africa*. Country Fact Files. Milwaukee: Raintree Steck-Vaughn, 1995.

Smith, Chris. *Conflict in Southern Africa*. Conflicts. New York: New Discovery, 1993.

South Africa in Pictures. Visual Geography. Minneapolis: Lerner Publications, 1988.

PICTURE ACKNOWLEDGMENTS:
The publishers would like to thank the following for allowing their photographs to be reproduced in this book: AKG London 11; Bruce Coleman 8, 9, 10, 22, 25, 26, 36; Camera Press 14 (bottom); Eye Ubiquitous 4, 6, 35, 38; Impact Photos *title page*, 7, 13, 14 (top), 19, 20, 21, 23, 31, 40–41, 42, 42–43; Panos Pictures *contents page*, 12, 16, 18, 27, 28, 29, 30, 33, 34, 37, 39; Telegraph Colour Library *cover;* Life File 41; Tony Stone Worldwide 24.

Index

Numbers in **bold** refer to photographs.

African National Congress
   (ANC) **12,** 13, 14, 46
apartheid 12, 13, 15, 30, 37, 46

Botswana 4

Cape Town 34, 38, 42
cattle 20, **20**
civil rights 4, 12, 13
climate 7, 8
clothing industry 29
coal 23
cola wars 30
cotton 18
countryside 15, 35
crops 7, 17, **17,** 18, 20, 36
   barley 17
   cereal 17
   corn 17, 18, 20, 36
   peanuts 20
   wheat 17, 18
currency 5

dams 17
desert 8, 9, 10
diamonds 22, 24, **24,** 44
Drakensburg Mountains **3,**
   6, **6,** 38
drought 7, **7,** 17
Durban 15, 27, 34, 42
Dutch East India Company
   11, 20

education 31, **31,** 32
electricity 23, 35, 44
environment 39

family planning 32
farming 16
   commercial 16, 17, 20
   subsistence 16
fishing 21, 27
forestry 20, 27
fruit 18

Germany 43
gold 11, 22, **22,** 23, **23,** 27,
   43, 44
Great Britain 11, 37, 43, 44
Great Escarpment 6

health 33
homelands 5, 12, 13, 46
   Ciskei 5
   Bophuthatswana 5
   Venda 5
   Transkei 5
housing 4, 34, **34,** 45
hydroelectricity 9, 29, 46

imports 43
industry 27–30
   clothing **28,** 29
   consumer goods 28–30
   engineering 28
   iron and steel 27, **27**
   plastics 29
infant mortality **32**
irrigation 9, 17, 18, 29, 46

Japan 43, 44
jobs 35, 45
Johannesburg *title page,* 22,
   29, 30, 34, 42

Kruger National Park **6,** 40,
   41

languages 4, 5, 10, **11,** 12,
   14, 46
Lesotho 4, 29

Mandela, Nelson 13, **13,** 14,
   14, 32
Maponya, Richard 30, **30**
markets 36, **36**
media 37
minerals 22, 44
mining 11, 22–26, **22, 23, 26,**
   27
Mozambique 4, 40, 42

Namibia 4
national parks 6, 39–41
nuclear power stations 23,
   44–45

ornamental plants 19

peoples
   Boers 11, **11**

British 11, 12
   Khoikhoi 10
   Nuguni 10, 46
   San 10, 46
   Sotho-Tswana 11
   Tsonga 11
   Venda 11
   Xhosa 10, **10**
   Zulu 10
population 5, 15
   density 15, **15**
   growth 29, 32, 44
   migration 15
power stations 23

radio 37
railroads 42, 44
reforestation 20
rivers 9
   Limpopo 11
   Orange 5, 9, **9,** 17, 18, 24
   Zambezi 10

settlers 6, 11, 12
sheep 17, 20, 36
sports 37
sugarcane 18, **18**
sugar plantations 12
Swaziland 4
Switzerland 43

Table Mountain *cover,* 38
television 37, **37**
tobacco 18
tourism 38, 39, **39,** 40–41, 46
townships 12, 30, 46
transportation 42, 43

United States 37, 43, 44

vegetation 8
volcanoes 24

weather 7
wildlife 8, 39
wine 19, **19**

Zimbabwe 4, 42

© Copyright 1996 Wayland (Publishers) Ltd.

```
968        Flint, David
FLI        South Africa
```

GAYLORD F